DONNA ERICKSON'S

Rainy Day

FUN BOOK

Illustrated by David LaRochelle

PARENT/TEACHER

PP

*To the memory of Uncle Carl Anduri,
who knew the secret of transforming ordinary things
into treasures.*

DONNA ERICKSON'S RAINY DAY FUN BOOK

Cover design by David Meyer
Cover photograph by Ann Marsden

Library of Congress Cataloging-in-Publication Data

Erickson, Donna
    Donna Erickson's rainy day fun book / by Donna Erickson ;
illustrated by David LaRochelle.
        p. cm. — (Prime time family series)
        ISBN 0-8066-2984-3 (alk. paper)
        1. Amusements. 2. Creative activities and seat work. I. Title. II. Series.
GV1229.E74 1996
793'.01'922—dc20   96-22558
                                                                          CIP

The paper used in this publication meets the minimum requirements of American National Standard for Information Sciences—Permanence of Paper for Printed Library Materials, ANSI Z329.48-1984.

∞

Manufactured in the U.S.A.   AF 9-2984

00 99 98 97 96   1 2 3 4 5 6 7 8 9 10

What's Inside

Notes from Donna

Weather the Storm—With a Smile

When the weather report sounds bleak, don't despair: there are dozens of indoor activities and learning experiences that can help you to weather the storm with a smile!

Cooking together. The kitchen is an exciting place for all ages. Where else can the sounds of clanging pots and pans, the whirling of beaters, and the aroma of mouth-watering food create such wonderful harmony? And cooking together can lead to creativity, scientific learning, discussions about nutrition, *and* delicious treats.

Making clothes and accessories. You don't have to be an expert tailor to take on the clothes and accessory projects in this book. If you have basic sewing skills and a willingness to try easy craft ideas, you're all set. Each of the suggestions is simple enough to involve your children, and they'll love the results.

Creating craft projects. It's a special moment when my kids present me with something they've made. Whether it's an imaginative finger painting, a paper-sculpture assemblage, or a colorful mobile, their faces beam from ear to ear when they declare, "I made it myself." Even if you don't consider yourself very "crafty," get involved in crafts with your children. You'll discover a relaxing diversion from your routine and a great chance to communicate, laugh, and share ideas together.

No matter how you choose to fill those bad-weather days, take advantage of the opportunity to snatch special moments with your kids. Whether you catch each other's undivided attention for a minute or an hour, these rainy-day interludes will fill the soul with meaning and pleasure. None of the activities will keep the socks sorted or the fridge stocked, but they will help make the time you spend with your kids count—and provide fun for everyone!

Weather the rainy days
with a smile!
Donna Erickson

5

Fun and Games

Television Bingo

As parents, we can hardly deny the influence TV has on children's lives. We need to take an active role in determining what and how much our children watch. Sometimes that means turning the TV off.

Viewing TV with our children and discussing what they see are positive steps toward balancing its influence on impressionable minds. And we can have fun if we turn the process into a game. Here's a takeoff on "Travel Bingo" that your family can play while viewing.

• Make TV Bingo cards by drawing grids on pieces of paper—5 squares across, 5 down.

• Take turns naming something you might see on a TV program: a dog, a man with a hat, a child on a bike, etc. Write these on the grid, one per square in a random fashion. Everyone should have a different arrangement.

• During the program, players check off items they spot on TV with a pencil. The first player to achieve a "bingo" wins.

TV Talk

If you and your kids become active viewers and critical thinkers, TV can both entertain and provide a chance to share ideas. Here are two ways to enhance your TV viewing.

• Make a chart listing days of the week down the left side. Make headings for columns across the top: number of programs watched, time spent, favorite and least favorite programs, etc. Fill in the chart regularly. Then use the chart to assess your viewing habits. If you're watching too much TV, do something about it. Begin by eliminating your least favorite shows. Talk about what you could do together instead of watching TV—then try out some of those ideas.

• Become active viewers. For example, watch one of your kids' favorite sitcoms with them and use the situations on TV as topics for discussion. Today's shows deal with all kinds of social and family issues that are ripe for sharing opinions.

The Memory Game

You will need: tagboard cut into 1 ½" squares
identical pairs of pictures, drawings, stickers, coupons, cut-outs from magazines, newspapers, canceled postage stamps and school photos
glue

Young children generally do better than adults when they play this memory game, which is made of pairs of cards that players must match (similar to the game show "Concentration"). Create a homemade game using stickers, pictures, and other funny things kids find around the house.

Not only do children feel a sense of success when they play, but they are also delighted when their own picture appears on the table!

To make the cards: Glue each item onto a tagboard square, making sure there are identical items to make a pair. You may make as many as 20 pairs, although if preschoolers are just learning the game you may wish to start with 5 to 10 pairs.

To play, shuffle the cards, and place them face down on a table in even rows of 5 cards each. To begin, the first player turns over one card. (When playing with preschoolers you may wish to say out loud what the card is, such as, "A sticker of a pink dinosaur." This helps to reinforce the image.) The player then turns over a second card. If it doesn't match, the player turns the two cards back over and the next player begins. If a player matches two cards, those cards are given to the player, and he or she takes another turn. Each person plays until he or she no longer makes a match.

The object of the game is to get the most matches—a feat often accomplished by a child!

Mini-Games and Puzzle Tips

• To help young children hold playing cards, make a card holder from two plastic coffee can lids and a brass paper fastener. Put the lids together, smooth sides facing, and connect in the middle with the paper fastener. Insert the playing cards between the two lids.

• Use empty, plastic 2-liter soft drink bottles and sponge balls for a fun bat and ball for toddlers. Or save several bottles and make a bowling game.

• Use a marker to write the same number or symbol on the backs of each piece of a younger child's puzzles. When it's time to pick up the puzzles, all pieces with the number "2" go in one box and all pieces with a "star" go in another box.

• Make a refrigerator puzzle for your preschooler. Glue flat magnets (available at craft or hardware stores) to the backs of large puzzle pieces from a 4 or 5 piece puzzle. Your child can put the puzzle together on the refrigerator door while you prepare a meal. The puzzle pieces can also be used as refrigerator magnets for artwork and notes your family displays.

Cookin' Up a Storm

Quick Munchies
for Little Munchers

There are a lot of expensive snack foods on the market these days, and small children are not immune to the professional marketing directed at them. How can you serve nutritious snacks without kids saying, "Not that! It's boring"? Jazz 'em up! Here are a couple of favorite ideas:

Create a smiling snack

You will need: 1 red apple
peanut butter
miniature marshmallows
(3 to 4 per snack)
paring knife

Quarter the apple and then cut each quarter in half to make two thin slices for each "smile." Spread peanut butter on one side of each slice. Line up miniature marshmallows in a row on the peanut butter side of one slice and top with the matching slice, peanut butter down. Makes 4 toothy smile snacks.

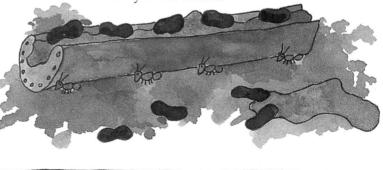

Ants on a log

You will need:

> 1 stalk of celery
> peanut butter
> raisins (4 to 5 per snack)

This snack is a favorite of a lot of kids. They won't mind inviting these "ants" to a picnic! Even very young children can help in the preparations.

Clean the celery and cut it into 3" pieces. Fill the hollow side of each celery piece with peanut butter. Arrange raisins on top of the peanut butter. Makes 3 to 4 snacks.

Pizzas with Pizzazz

You will need: pre-made pizza dough (or your
favorite recipe)
favorite toppings for kids, such
as grated cheese, sausage,
ground beef, and mush-
rooms
tomato sauce
flour
pastry brush
bread board
pizza pan or cookie sheet

It's hard to find a kid who doesn't like pizza. A winner for party eats, Saturday night suppers, and after-school snacks, pizza is as fun to make as it is good to eat. Here's a version to try at your child's next birthday party. While the personal pizzas are baking, the birthday boy or girl can open gifts, or the guests can play games. When the sizzling pizzas come out of the oven, everyone will be excited to taste their own culinary creations.

Divide the dough into individual portions and form each into a ball. Store each ball in an airtight container or under a plastic covering until ready to use. Prepare toppings and place them in individual bowls.

Preheat oven to 350°. Let each child roll out the dough on a floured bread board to make a 5" to 6" round. Lift the dough onto a cookie sheet or pizza pan. Brush tomato sauce on the dough and add toppings according to taste. Bake pizzas for 15 to 20 minutes. Serve with fresh fruit or a green salad.

Fresh Fruit with a Twist

You will need: a fresh pineapple cut in half
lengthwise
a variety of other fruit, such
as mangos, bananas, grapes,
strawberries, blueberries,
lemons, shredded coconut,
and raisins

Including kids in food preparations is one of the most natural ways to provide a pinch of learning at mealtime. Measuring, pouring, stirring, and observing chemical reactions in a mixing bowl is exciting stuff for curious, growing minds. While educators refer to

such activities as "teachable moments," there is more than instruction going on. When we spend uninterrupted time with our kids, we are building both skills and relationships. Here's a cheery rainy-day recipe you and your kids can make together. Serve it in an unusual bowl they'll love—a half shell of a pineapple! As you prepare the salad, stir up learning, too, with the questions below.

Set out a variety of ripe fruit. Then ask your children to name each. Which is largest? Smallest? Which fruit is your favorite? How are raisins made? How many do you want in the salad? Count them and set them aside.

An adult should slice the pineapple in half lengthwise. Cut the fruit from the halves. Save the pineapple shells and place the cut-up fruit in a mixing bowl. As you work, ask: "How does a pineapple grow and where?"

Wash, peel, and cut the rest of the ingredients, adding them to the mixing bowl. Squeeze and drizzle lemon juice over the fruit. Ask, "What does drizzle mean?"

Scoop the fruit mixture into the pineapple halves. As you complete the luscious salad, ask, "Why is a fruit salad healthy? What else could we put in a pineapple fruit salad next time?"

Inside Science

Cave in a Jar

You will need: 2 small glass jars, such as
baby food jars, with labels removed
6 teaspoons of baking soda
1 large, disposable plastic plate
glue
1 length of wool yarn, 14"
hot water
magnifying glass

The visit to a real cave with stalactites and stalagmites is breathtaking. Here's a science activity that will let you observe stalactites and stalagmites forming on your own turf.

Keep the jars secure by gluing them, 3 to 4 inches apart, onto the plate. Fill the jars with hot water. Stir 3 teaspoons of baking soda into each jar. Set the plate on a shelf or table where the jars won't be disturbed.

Put the ends of the yarn in the solution in each jar, allowing yarn to hang between the jars without touching the plate. After several days, observe stalagmites forming on the plate and stalactites forming on the yarn. Use a magnifying glass to observe the formations during early stages.

Here's how it works: The baking soda-and-water solution travels up the yarn and drips onto the plate. The water evaporates, leaving the baking soda in a pile, forming the stalagmites. Baking soda on the yarn forms stalactites. In underground caves, the formations develop from minerals dissolved in slowly dripping water.

For extra fun, make cave drawings on a piece of paper cut from a recycled brown grocery bag. Use colors from nature to brighten the artwork by rubbing nontoxic plants, such as geranium petals or blades of grass, on the drawings. Hang the cave drawings behind the experiment.

Growing Rocks to Eat

You will need: 1 heat-resistant clear drinking
glass or canning jar
1 cup of water
3 to 3 ½ cups of sugar
clean string
pencil

Here's a fun indoor activity that will teach your family about crystal formation. Since sugar crystal formation can take up to two weeks, your children will learn a bit about patience, too. But when they observe candy forming on the string, even youngsters with short attention spans will hang in there.

An adult should boil one cup of water in a saucepan. Start adding sugar a few tablespoons at a time. Stir as the sugar dissolves and a syrup forms. Keep an eye on the pan at all times so the syrup doesn't boil over. Turn down the heat if necessary. When all of the sugar is dissolved and the syrup is clear, remove from heat and let cool for about 10 minutes. Pour into the glass or jar.

Meanwhile, let the kids cut three 10" lengths of string. Tie one end of each piece around the middle of a pencil, leaving a little space between each string. An adult should rest the pencil across the rim of the glass or jar and lower the strings into the syrup. Adjust the strings so they don't touch the bottom.

Set the glass or jar in a safe place in easy view of the children. Check on it daily, but don't disturb it. If crystals cover the top of the sugar-water solution, carefully break up the crust with a spoon to let evaporation continue. Wait patiently, and in about two weeks you should have rock candy!

Egghead Garden

You will need: 1 empty eggshell with the
top ¼ broken off
1 egg cup or small napkin ring
3 damp cotton balls
⅛ teaspoon alfalfa seeds
fine-tipped felt markers

This miniature gardening activity is especially fun for preschool gardeners.

After breaking off the top ¼ of an eggshell,
gently rinse it out with warm water. When it is
thoroughly dry, use colored markers to draw a
face on the eggshell. A child's self-portrait is
especially fun. Display the shell in an egg cup
or napkin ring.

Place damp cotton balls inside the eggshell.
Sprinkle seeds over the cotton and keep these
damp. In two or three days, the seeds will
begin to sprout. Put the egghead garden in a
sunny spot.

As the sprouts grow, your child can give the
egghead a "haircut." Sprinkle the nutritious
clippings on a salad, or add to a sandwich at
lunchtime.

Paperwork Projects

Wad a Masterpiece!

You will need: several sheets of brightly colored tissue
paper, cut into ½" x 16" strips
12" x 16" white art paper or construction
paper
paper cup
white school glue (water soluble)
artist paintbrush
newspaper
sequins, glitter, small beads (optional)

This is perfect for a preschooler's first art project!

Pour just enough glue into the paper cup to cover the bottom, and add about ¼ cup water. Mix thoroughly. Cover your work surface with newspaper, and lay out white paper, glue mixture, tissue-paper strips, and a paintbrush.

Using the paintbrush, "paint" the glue solution on the art paper—the more glue, the better—then crumple up strips of tissue paper in a variety of colors and press the wads onto the art paper. Add more glue solution whenever needed. Once satisfied with the picture, set it aside to dry. Let the young artist sign the masterpiece with first name or initials, then display it at home, or frame it for the office as a colorful reminder of your child's creativity.

For a variation, sprinkle some sequins, colored beads, and glitter on the glue—you'll have fireworks going in all directions!

Stuffed with Color

You will need: acetate (sold by the yard
at art-supply and stationery
stores; 1 yard will make
several shapes)
brightly colored tissue paper,
cut into ½" x 12" strips
stapler
scissors
felt-tipped permanent markers
ribbon or string (optional)

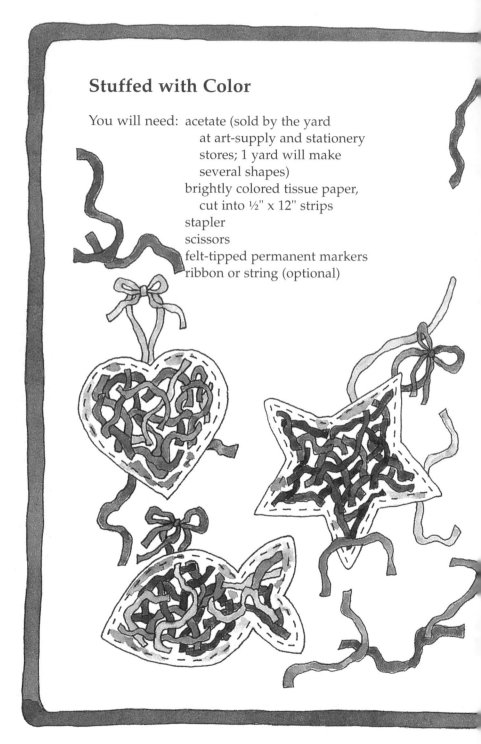

Add a splash of color to your home or office with this art project. Make a fish to hang in Dad's office if he is a biology teacher or an avid sportsman. Make an airplane for a frequent flyer. Or make a bright pink and red heart to hang in your window for Valentine's Day. Whatever you choose to create, the final product will be an eye-catcher.

Fold the acetate in half to make a double layer. With a permanent marker, draw the shape of the figure on the acetate. Cut out both layers for two identical pieces.

Staple the two pieces together along the outside edge, spacing the staples every ¼". Leave a 2" opening. Stuff the acetate shape with tissue-paper strips. Continue stuffing until all corners and curves have been filled. Staple the opening shut. Staple ribbon or string to the top of the figure for hanging.

Puff Paint and Paper

You will need: 1 cup white flour
1 cup salt
1 cup water
tempera paint
plastic squeeze bottle
construction paper
glitter (optional)

Kids can create a "puffy" effect when painting on paper by using the following recipe. It's inexpensive, easy to mix, and virtually mess-less because the paint is applied with a squeeze bottle. It "puffs" on its own as it dries.

In a small mixing bowl, stir together the flour, salt, and water. Add several teaspoons of tempera paint. Stir. Pour into a clean honey bear or other plastic squeeze bottle. On a newspaper-covered work surface, squeeze paint onto the paper. Add glitter while the paint is still wet for added sparkle. For the best results, use the paint up within two or three days.

Note: This painting project is enjoyable for visually impaired children. When the paint dries, they can feel their designs with their hands. Do not use this paint on fabric.

The Big Frame-up

You will need: mat board (available at craft
or art stores)
art clips (available at office-
supply stores)
wooden embroidery hoop
(available at craft stores)
second-hand frames (check
garage sales!)

If your refrigerator door is overloaded with your children's art, poetry, or awards, try some of these inexpensive and easy framing ideas for attractive displays. Before you begin, write the date and your child's name on the back of projects you save.

1. For small- to medium-sized drawings or poems, use a wooden embroidery hoop. Center the smaller hoop under the piece and bring the hoops together as you would with needlework. Trim off the extra paper around the edge, and hang on the wall.

2. To display larger projects, make a revolving frame. Purchase mat board cut to the exact size of the piece, or you can buy precut standard-size matting. Center the project behind the mat board and clip the layers together at the top with colorful spring clips. Place the matted piece on a plate rack for displaying on your hutch, mantel, or bookcase. Because the art is attached to the matting with clips, it may be easily removed when a new project is brought home to take its place.

3. Renovate second-hand frames you pick up at garage sales. Clean and paint these, using leftover wall or stencil paint from the room in which the art will hang. Take your frame to a frame shop where you can get matting cut to size. Mount the artwork and hang it where it will get the most raves!

Musical Madness

Milk Carton Guitar

You will need: a clean, empty half-gallon cardboard
milk carton with the top taped shut
wooden yardstick
45" to 50" of nylon fishing line

You can really make music with this simple home-made guitar!

Cut notches about ½" deep near each end of the yardstick. Cut vertical slits on two sides of the milk carton ⅔ up from the bottom. Insert the yardstick through the slits, positioning the carton near the center of the yardstick. Make a loop in one end of the fishing line and slip it over the notch on one end of the yardstick. Pull the line over the top of the carton and loop it around the notch at the other end of the yardstick. Tie and knot it securely.

To play the instrument, strum the string near the bridge (the top edge of the milk carton) with one hand. Pinch the string to the yardstick with the other hand to change pitches. Adjust the position of the carton, if necessary. Your kids may soon discover that the numbers printed on the yardstick can be helpful in locating the pitch they need for a song.

Pie Plate Rhythm

You will need: 1 foil or tin pie plate
6 to 8 flattened bottle caps
string
ice pick

Here's an instrument that is easy to make and fun to play when kids want to accentuate the rhythm of a band!

Using the ice pick, an adult should make 6 to 8 holes around the edge of the pie plate and one hole in each bottle cap. Let the children pull a piece of string through a bottle cap and a hole in the pie plate, making tight knots to hold the bottle cap in place. Be sure to allow enough slack in the string so the cap can move freely and hit the pie plate when it is shaken. Continue this procedure until all caps are attached. Then give it a good shake—you're ready to play!

Bottle Blowin' Blues

You will need: several empty, same-size
                bottles, such as soda pop
                or mineral water bottles
                pitcher filled with water

    This activity works well for musical solos,
but it's even more fun with duets. So gather
the materials you'll need, grab a partner, and
blow a tune!
    Line up the bottles and pour a different
amount of water into each one, starting with a
small amount in the first and gradually
increasing the amount until one bottle is
nearly full. Tune the bottles by blowing into
them and emptying or adding water to
achieve the pitch you desire. Try playing a
familiar tune or make up something new.

Ready to Wear— With Flair

Hair's the Thing

You will need: colorful fabric, 4" wide by
18" long
elastic strip, ½" wide by 9" long
safety pin, straight pins
needle and thread
grosgrain or satin ribbon for hair bow
decorative button, silk rosette,
or charm
hair clip, hair comb, or headband
glue
fishing line (optional)

Enjoy creative fun when you embellish ordinary clips, headbands, and ribbons for colorful hair accessories.

Perky ponytail holder. With right sides facing, fold the fabric strip in half lengthwise. Pin edges together along the length and sew, allowing ½" seam. Remove pins. Turn the fabric tube right side out and, with adult assistance, press.

STITCH, THEN TURN
FABRIC TUBE RIGHT
← SIDE OUT

TIE OR SEW
ELASTIC ENDS
← TOGETHER

THEN →
STITCH
TOGETHER
THE FABRIC ENDS

Pin a safety pin to one end of the elastic and push through the tube. Remove the pin. Tie the elastic ends together in a knot or stitch them together. Stitch the fabric ends together, making sure all raw edges are folded under.

Highlight a bow. Tie a bow with grosgrain or satin ribbon. Try special wired ribbon, manufactured to help keep the bow's shape. Sew a decorative button or glue a silk rosette or charm on the knot. Glue the bow to the top side of a hair clip, hair comb, or headband. For added strength, wind and knot fishing wire around the bow and accessory.

Accessory Hints

• Keep ribbons from falling off a ponytail or braid by tying the ribbon to an elastic band before wrapping the band around your hair. Once the band is in place, tie the ribbon in a bow.

• When youngsters make ponytails on their dolls, use a wire twist tie or plastic closure from a bread bag instead of a rubber band. Children can usually do this themselves.

Patch-ups

You will need: fabric scraps or fabric with
prints of favorite storybook or
cartoon characters
pins, needle, thread
polyfill
pieces of hook and loop
fastener, such as Velcro brand
small bows or cloth flowers
ribbons, buttons, lace

If you've noticed that your preschooler's favorite sweatpants are threadbare at the knees, here's an easy way to give them new life and a bit of whimsy. Enlist your child's help with this "patch-up" project.

Dig through your fabric scraps with your child and choose a design or pattern that will look good on the worn pants. Or buy about ⅛ yard of fabric.

Cut out two patches that will amply cover the knees of the pants, allowing an extra ⅝" on all sides. Fold edges back ⅝" and press the fold with a hot iron. Pin the patches to the knees and then stitch around the patch, leaving a 1" opening. Remove pins and press. Stuff a handful of polyfill through the opening. The extra padding will add comfort and protect knees and pants. Stitch the patch closed. Repeat on the other leg of the pants.

If your child has a plain, matching sweatshirt, applique a coordinating design or character on the bodice. Embellish with ribbons, buttons, or lace.

For example, if you use a clown, stitch a piece of Velcro on the clown's hair. Sew matching pieces of fastener on several bows or cloth flowers. Your child will enjoy choosing a different bow or flower to accessorize the clown for any occasion.

Pearls of Pasta

You will need: a variety of shapes, sizes
and colors of pasta, such
as spirals, bows, and
tubes
colored wooden beads
poster or acrylic paints
(metallic colors are
especially dazzling)
shoelaces, string, ribbon,
or elastic

Have you noticed that basic noodles have become updated? What was once maco-cheese is now marketed as fettuccini alfredo. And when it comes to arts and crafts, kids no longer make macaroni necklaces and bracelets. They string pasta jewelry.

To make your own jewelry, cover your work surface with newspaper. Then sort out the shapes you want to paint and give them a coat of color.

String the pasta shapes alternately with beads. For variety, thread the string through two shapes, then up through the first before going on to the next shape.

If your string is too thick to go through the pasta bows, simply glue the bows onto pasta tubes and string the tubes onto the necklace.

To make bracelets, thread pasta and beads on elastic. For a jazzy pin, glue several shapes together and attach a clasp to the back.

Cozy Cover-up for Bath Time

You will need: 1 bath towel
 1 fingertip towel
 pins, thread
 button or a 2" strip of hook and loop
  fastener, such as Velcro brand
  (optional)
 sewing machine

Sew a fingertip towel to a colorful bath towel and your child will have a clever cover-up that can be used every time he or she gets out of the tub or a swimming pool. When you see how easy it is to make, you'll want to make more for baby shower and birthday gifts.

Fold the fingertip towel in half with right sides facing, and stitch along one side, allowing a ½" seam allowance. Turn right-side out. Find and mark the center point on one of the long edges of the bath towel. Mark the center point on the unsewn length of the fingertip towel. Match the bath towel and fingertip towel at the marked points and pin the towels together, right sides facing. Stitch from one end of the fingertip towel to the other. Remove pins. Fit the hooded towel on your child. For a front closure, stitch strips of Velcro to the bath towel or make a buttonhole and sew on a button.

SEW SEW

Measuring Up

Chore Challenge Chart

You will need: a sheet of poster board
crayons or markers
one medium-sized envelope for
each child
disks cut from plastic coffee can
lids, or checkers or pieces from an old
game

There are numerous ways you can weave activities into your family life to promote confidence in your kids. One of the most basic is giving them chores to do, starting with your preschoolers. This chore chart works as a simple incentive system for all ages—readers and non-readers alike.

Lay a sheet of poster board horizontally on the table. Let children write their names in a column down the left side of the board. Allow 5" between each name. If your child doesn't read, glue a photo next to his or her name.

Use a yardstick to draw a line extending across the board under each name. Then draw vertical lines to make a grid. Make enough spaces for the number of chores the child should perform. Allow for two extra spaces on the right side.

Cut off the top flap of the envelopes and staple one at the end of each child's row.

Next to the child's name, write a chore in each box on that row of the grid. For non-readers, draw a simple sketch to illustrate the chore. In each box where a chore is written/drawn, draw a circle or two or three (representing plastic disks or tokens) to indicate the number of points the child will receive for completing the chore.

Hang the chart low enough so your child can see it. Each time the child performs a task, place the appropriate number of tokens (as indicated on the chart) in his or her envelope. When a predetermined number of tokens is accumulated, reward your child by doing something special together.

A Bookworm Board

You will need: a large sheet of poster board
felt-tipped markers in a variety
of colors
stickers (optional)

		10 min	15 min				150 min. =
MONDAY		10 min	15 min				
TUESDAY		15 min	10 min				
WEDNESDAY		5 min					
THURSDAY		20 min					
FRIDAY		10 min					
SATURDAY		15					
SUNDAY							

Challenge your school-age children to read with a reading progress chart. You'll have fun making the chart together, and the children will look forward to filling in each day to reach their goal—and their reward!

Lay the poster board horizontally on your work surface. Have your child draw a long, squiggly bookworm across the top. Then draw a large grid on the rest of the poster board. Print the days of the week along the left side of the grid (see illustration). Decide on some goals and rewards together.

Chart reading progress by recording the number of minutes read each day or the number of pages read. When the goal is reached, reward the children with something for which they were aiming, such as a new book, an ice-cream cone, or a pizza outing.

All children benefit from being read to. Adapt this activity by recording the number of books you and your child read together. Reward both child and adult by doing something special together!

Thumbs-up Growth Chart

You will need: a sheet of plain white butcher
or shelf paper (3 feet long)
measuring tape
marker, pencil, or pen
stickers or photos of child
(optional)
ink pad or poster paint

Your kids are growing all the time. You see it in photos in the family album, and the kids feel it when they try on last year's clothes—now too short or too tight.

Although growing happens gradually, your kids can watch themselves grow with these simple measuring activities on a growth chart. Here's how:

Spread the shelf paper on the floor. Mark the bottom right edge with a line and label it "24 inches." Mark the bottom left edge with a line labeled "2 feet."

Use the measuring tape along the length of the paper to mark off 1-inch segments going up the right side of the paper. End at the top of the sheet with "60 inches." Be sure to mark the left side with corresponding number of feet. Spruce up the chart with drawings, stickers, or photos, if you wish.

Hang the measuring chart on a wall or on your child's closet door, 2 feet up from the floor. Measure your child's height and note it on the chart along with the date. Now have your child get on a scale and record his or her weight next to the height. For extra fun, use an ink pad or poster paint to make a thumb print next to the other notations.

Every six months, let your child mark his or her height, weight, thumbprint, and the date on the chart. Kids may be surprised to discover they didn't grow much during some periods and grew a lot during others.

In the meantime, remind your kids to eat well, get plenty of exercise, get lots of sleep, and keep on growing!

Let's Pretend

Costume Treasure Box

You will need: a large box
old clothing, such as hats, dresses,
scarves, shoes, shirts, and purses

Children love dressing up and pretending they are Mom, Dad, or a host of imaginative characters. Stimulate their play by putting together a costume box. It will also come in handy for last-minute costumes for trick-or-treating, if your family celebrates Halloween.

Start your collection with old dresses and suits. If you don't have a used bridesmaid's dress or Hawaiian shirt hanging in the back of your closet, look for them at garage and estate sales. You'll probably find some funny hats, costume jewelry, and elbow-length gloves along the way!

Here are some basic items to get you and your kids started: large scarves, party and professional hats (firefighter, baseball player, nurse, etc.), costume jewelry, dresses, shirts, nightgowns, vests, wigs, boots, slippers, shoes, purses, backpacks, small suitcases, large piece of cloth for capes, shawls and stage curtains.

Once your costume box is full of props and disguises, you'll find it invaluable for entertaining children on a rainy or cold day, and ideal for costuming kids for amateur productions and masquerade parties.

Make-a-Face Paint

You will need: 1 teaspoon corn starch
½ teaspoon water
½ teaspoon cold cream
food coloring (variety of colors)
small yogurt container, clean
and dry (one for each color paint)
small paintbrush

Face painting done in creative shapes and designs is a nice alternative to wearing a mask on Halloween (masks can be frightening to preschoolers, and they may obscure vision). In addition, kids will enjoy this recipe for birthday parties, staging a backyard play, and for dress-up on a rainy day.

The process of making homemade face paint will give a school-age child a valuable experience in following directions, measuring ingredients, and combining and experimenting with colors.

Stir together the corn starch and cold cream until well-blended. Add water and stir. Add food coloring, a drop at a time, until you get the desired color. Experiment with the colors by adding more drops of the same color for a darker paint or by adding a different color to create a new shade. Three drops of blue and one drop of green food coloring will create turquoise. Two drops of yellow and one drop of red blends into orange. Two drops of blue and one drop of red will make violet. Paint designs on faces with a small paintbrush; remove with soap and water. The face paint may be stored in covered yogurt containers.

Tub-Bubble Beards

You will need: wet washcloth
               bar of hand soap

Nothing can top this bathtub activity for laughs and fun!

Rub hand soap generously on one side of a very wet washcloth. Hold the washcloth up to your mouth with the soapy side facing away from you. Blow gently through the washcloth. As you blow, a magnificent bubble beard will begin to grow on the washcloth. If you keep blowing, the beard will drape several inches and become fuller and fuller. Add more water to the washcloth or more soap if necessary. When the kids want to make their own bubble beards, caution them to blow through the washcloth, instead of inhaling.

Rainy Day
Odds and Ends

Activities for Preschoolers

When bad weather keeps your preschoolers indoors, here's a list of activities to stir up some creative fun.

• Unravel a ball of string and wind it through your house. Tell your children to follow it from the starting point to a surprise snack at the end.

• Gather a dozen small, familiar items, such as a rubber ball, comb, sponge, sheet of tissue paper, grape, etc. and place them in a paper bag. Ask your child to put his or her hand into the bag and try to identify each item, one at a time, without looking.

• Thumb through photo albums and shoe boxes with your children and look for their baby pictures. Tell anecdotes about the kids when they were younger. Show children your baby pictures, too.

• Make a pint-size "office" or "craft center." Use a large, sturdy cardboard box for a desk. Remove the top flaps of the box or fold them inside, and place the box on its side. Scoot a small chair in front of the open end. Let your child paint designs on the box. Cover empty frozen juice cans with colorful adhesive-backed paper to hold pens, markers, and child-safe scissors. Tuck scrap paper, construction paper, and old magazines in a shoe box for art supplies.

• Go on a "geometry safari" in your house and categorize objects by their shape. For example, the sofa pillow may be a square, the clock a circle, the lampshade a triangle, etc.

• Choose a favorite storybook or two from the bookshelf. Read the first half aloud and create a different ending together.

• At bedtime, ask your children what they did today that they are proud of. For example, "I put my boots on by myself," or "I made a birthday card for Grandpa."

Dial-a-Picture Phone Book

You will need: 3" x 5" notecards or pieces of
plain paper
pictures of children's friends
felt-tipped markers or crayons
paper punch
ribbon string

Your kids can make their own phone directory even if they aren't readers. On notecards, glue school pictures or draw pictures of friends and family your kids might call. Next to the picture, print the person's name and telephone number in large, clear letters. You might add emergency numbers by appropriate pictures. Your kids can keep their special directory next to the phone with the city phone book.

Discuss phone rules and etiquette with young children. They should understand that the phone is not a toy and should only be used with permission. For older children, discuss etiquette, including the maximum length of calls, appropriate times for calling people, and the correct way to answer the phone.

My Family Picture Book

You will need: 3 sheets of 9" x 12" colored
                construction paper
           1 roll of clear, adhesive-backed
              paper
           glue
           felt-tipped markers in a variety
              of colors
           paper punch
           1 yard of ribbon
           12 photos of different family
              members, including one of
              your child

With relatives often living many miles apart, it can be hard to maintain close contact with cousins, aunts and uncles, and grandparents. To keep your young child familiar with the faces of important people in his or her life, make a personal picture book.

Because the pages will be protected with clear adhesive-backed paper, peanut butter and other sticky stuff can easily be removed with a damp cloth. And when the relatives arrive for the holidays, your child will probably be the first to call them by name even though they have not seen each other in ages.

Cut each sheet of construction paper in half. Glue a photo to the front and back side of the paper. Under each photo, use markers to print the name of the person in large letters.

Cut six 9" x 12" pieces of clear adhesive-backed paper. Cover each sheet of paper, folding the adhesive-backed construction paper around the right edge of the construction paper to make a durable page. Punch two holes on the left side of each page. Pile the six pages on top of each other, with your child's photo on top. Attach the pages together with a piece of string or ribbon tied through the two holes.

Make additional picture books using other topics. For example, a book called "My Neighborhood" could feature your house, car, park, library, etc.

Indoor Outings

Even if bad weather keeps you indoors, you don't have to stay at home. Here are great ways to spend indoor time with your kids—and still get out of the house!

• Note things that fascinate your child. Is he or she enamored with dinosaurs, castles and knights, horses, or even snakes? Match up their interests with an outing to a local museum, zoo, or library. Check your newspaper for special exhibits and programs.

• How about taking in a good family or kids' movie? Matinee prices are usually lower, and you can top off the film with a discussion over an ice-cream sundae afterward.

• Have your children ever visited the neighborhood where you grew up? Take them on a tour through your past—it'll be fun for you and instructive for the kids. Pack snacks or make a snack stop at one of your favorite childhood restaurants. As you pass old haunts, share stories of your early years.

• If you have preteen or junior high kids, take an educational trip to an indoor shopping mall. Before you go, hand out small notebooks or sheets of paper and let each person list one item to shop for, along with the price he or she expects to pay. Talk about and list what you will look for in the purchases: color, size, brand, style, comfort, etc. Then head for the mall and do group comparative shopping.

As you move from store to store, note the differences in price, selection, etc. Before you purchase anything, sit down over a cup of hot chocolate or soda, share discoveries, and make your decisions. This is a great way to teach children the value of careful shopping and good money management.

Parents' Page

Rainy Day Reading Tips

Perhaps no other skill pays greater dividends than the ability to read well. One of the best ways to encourage this skill—and a love for reading—in our children is by reading together as a family.

• To encourage reading, read aloud to your child. Even preteens will enjoy a story read to them now and then.

• Read stories and books with expression and slowly enough to allow your child to build mental pictures of the setting and action.

• Read at home with your child on your lap or snuggled against you in a cozy chair.

• Carry books wherever you go with your kids. A favorite story helps pass the time and quiets nerves while you wait in the doctor's or dentist's office.

• Make the local library a familiar place for your family. Many community libraries offer free activities for children, from story hours, puppet shows, and crafts, to reading incentive programs in the summertime.

• Designate a special shelf or basket in your home for borrowed library books. Replenish the supply regularly.

• Rediscover poetry. Select short poems at first, geared to your child's interest. Recite poems you remember from childhood. Write poems with your child. Put your original poems on cards, illustrate them, and make extra-special greeting cards.